Missouri

preface

Welcome to St. Louis, Missouri! As a lifelong resident of this vibrant city, I've had the privilege of witnessing its transformation over the past 25 years. From its historic landmarks to its burgeoning arts scene, St. Louis has captured my heart and continues to inspire me.

I've created this guide with the hope of sharing my love for St. Louis with you. Whether you're a seasoned traveler or a first-time visitor, I believe this city has something unique to offer everyone. From exploring iconic attractions like the Gateway Arch to discovering hidden gems in local neighborhoods, there's always something new to experience. My goal is to provide you with a practical and informative guide that will help you make the most of your time in St. Louis.

Whether you're planning a day trip, a weekend getaway, or a longer vacation, this book will offer suggestions for things to see, do, and eat. I hope that by the time you finish reading this guide, you'll be as excited as I am to explore the wonderful city of St. Louis. So let's dive in and discover all that this amazing place has to offer!

F.B. Daniels

table of contents

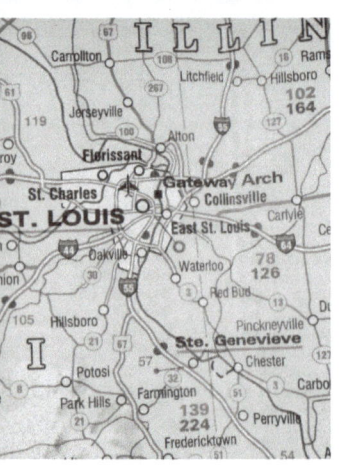

table of contents

Introduction

A Gateway to History and Culture

St. Louis, Missouri, a city steeped in history and brimming with cultural offerings, is a captivating destination for travelers seeking a unique blend of the old and the new. Nestled along the banks of the Mississippi River, St. Louis has played a pivotal role in the nation's development, serving as a gateway to the West and a hub for industry and commerce.

The city's rich history is evident in its iconic landmarks, such as the Gateway Arch, a soaring monument commemorating the westward expansion of the United States. Visitors can explore the city's past at the Old Courthouse, where the Dred Scott case was tried, and delve into the industrial heritage at the Anheuser-Busch Brewery, home of the world-famous Budweiser beer.

St. Louis' vibrant culture is reflected in its diverse neighborhoods, each with its own unique character and charm. From the historic Soulard district to the bustling Delmar Loop, visitors can experience a variety of culinary delights, arts and entertainment, and shopping opportunities. The city's commitment to the arts is evident in its world-class museums, theaters, and music venues, offering a wide range of cultural experiences.With its stunning architecture, beautiful parks, and friendly locals, St. Louis offers something for everyone. Whether you're a history buff, a foodie, or simply seeking a relaxing getaway, this charming city is sure to leave a lasting impression.

Why St. Louis is a Must-Visit Destination

St. Louis, Missouri, often overlooked by travelers, is a hidden gem that offers a unique blend of history, culture, and natural beauty. With its iconic landmarks, vibrant neighborhoods, and diverse culinary scene, St. Louis is a must-visit destination for anyone seeking an unforgettable experience.

Here's why St. Louis should be on your travel list:
- Iconic Landmarks: The Gateway Arch, a symbol of American expansion, dominates the city's skyline. Explore the Old Courthouse, where the Dred Scott case was tried, and visit the Anheuser-Busch Brewery for a tour and tasting.
- Vibrant Neighborhoods: Discover the historic charm of Soulard, the Grand Center district, or the trendy Delmar

Loop. Each neighborhood offers unique shops, restaurants, and cultural attractions.

- Diverse Culinary Scene: Indulge in St. Louis-style barbecue, gooey butter cake, and toasted ravioli. Explore the city's thriving craft beer scene or savor fine dining experiences.
- Cultural Attractions: Immerse yourself in the city's rich cultural heritage by visiting world-class museums, theaters, and music venues. Don't miss the St. Louis Zoo, the Missouri Botanical Garden, or the City Museum.
- Outdoor Adventures: Enjoy outdoor activities like hiking, biking, and boating in Forest Park, one of the largest urban parks in the United States. Explore the Mississippi Riverfront or visit nearby wineries.

Whether you're a history buff, a foodie, or simply seeking a relaxing getaway, St. Louis has something to offer everyone. This insider's guide will help you discover the hidden gems and must-see attractions that make St. Louis a truly unforgettable destination.

Getting to St. Louis: Your Transportation Options

St. Louis Lambert International Airport (STL) is the primary airport serving the St. Louis metropolitan area. It is located approximately 15 miles west of downtown St. Louis and is served by major airlines with both domestic and international flights.

Train: Amtrak provides service to St. Louis. The St. Louis Union Station is the main train station in the city, located downtown.

Bus: Greyhound Lines offers bus service to St. Louis, with the St. Louis Bus Station located downtown.

Car: If you're driving to St. Louis, major highways like Interstate 70, Interstate 44, and Interstate 64 intersect in the city. There are also several major highways leading to St. Louis from surrounding states.

Once in St. Louis:
Public Transportation: MetroLink is the light rail system that serves St. Louis and its suburbs. It connects major attractions, including the Gateway Arch, Forest Park, and the downtown area.
Taxis and Rideshare Services: Taxis and ride-sharing services like Uber and Lyft are readily available in St. Louis.

Rental Cars: Car rental agencies are located at the airport and throughout the city.

Choosing the Best Option:
The best way to get to St. Louis depends on your starting point, budget, and travel preferences. Consider factors such as flight times, train schedules, and the distance you'll be traveling.

The Best Time To Visit St. Louis

The best time to visit Sr. Louis depends on your preferences for weather and events. Here's a breakdown of the seasons:
Spring (March-May):

- Weather: Pleasant temperatures with occasional showers.
- Events: St. Patrick's Day Parade, Shakespeare Festival, Missouri Botanical Garden's Flower Festival.

Summer (June-August):
- Weather: Hot and humid, with occasional thunderstorms.
- Events: St. Louis Blues Hockey Playoffs, Cardinals Baseball Games, Shakespeare Festival, Fair St. Louis (Independence Day celebration).

Fall (September-November):
- Weather: Mild temperatures with colorful foliage.
- Events: St. Louis Art Fair, Missouri Botanical Garden's Fall Festival, St. Louis Blues Hockey Season.

Winter (December-February):
- Weather: Cold with occasional snow.
- Events: Winterfest at Forest Park, St. Louis Blues Hockey Season, New Year's Eve celebrations.

Consider these factors when choosing the best time to visit:
- Weather preference: If you prefer warmer weather, summer is a good option. If you enjoy cooler temperatures, spring or fall are ideal.
- Events: If you're interested in specific events, plan your trip accordingly.
- Budget: Prices for hotels and flights may be higher during peak tourist seasons (summer and fall).

Overall, spring and fall are generally considered the best times to visit St. Louis, offering pleasant weather and a variety of events.

Gateway Arch National Park

Gateway Arch National Park is a must-visit destination in St. Louis, offering breathtaking views of the city and the Mississippi River. The iconic Gateway Arch, a soaring stainless steel monument, stands as a symbol of America's westward expansion.

The Gateway Arch was designed by Eero Saarinen and was completed in 1965. It is the tallest man-made monument in the Western Hemisphere, standing at 630 feet (192 meters) tall. The Arch commemorates the westward expansion of the United States, which began in St. Louis.

Before ascending to the top of the Arch, visitors can explore the Museum at the Gateway Arch. The museum offers interactive exhibits that delve into the history of westward expansion, the construction of the Arch, and the cultural significance of the Mississippi River. Visitors can learn about the pioneers who traveled west, the challenges they faced, and the impact they had on the nation.

One of the most popular experiences at Gateway Arch National Park is taking the tram to the top of the Arch. The tram travels through a narrow, curved tunnel to the observation deck at the top, offering panoramic views of St. Louis and the surrounding region. On a clear day, visitors can see for miles, taking in the beauty of the Mississippi River, the city's skyline, and the surrounding countryside.

After visiting the Gateway Arch, be sure to explore some of the nearby attractions:

Old Courthouse: This historic building served as the federal courthouse for the St. Louis area and was the site of the famous Dred Scott case. Visitors can tour the courthouse and learn about its significant role in American history.

Mississippi River: Take a stroll along the Mississippi Riverfront and enjoy the scenic views. There are several parks and green spaces along the river, perfect for picnicking, biking, or simply relaxing.

Gateway Arch National Park is a must-see destination for anyone visiting St. Louis. With its iconic Arch, fascinating museum, and stunning views, it offers a unique and unforgettable experience.

Forest Park: A Green Oasis in the City

Forest Park is one of the largest urban parks in the United States, spanning over 1,300 acres in the heart of St. Louis. This beautiful green space offers a variety of attractions, from world-class museums to stunning gardens and recreational activities.

Forest Park was established in 1876 and has since become a beloved destination for both locals and visitors. The park features a variety of landscapes, including meadows, forests, lakes, and streams. Visitors can enjoy walking or biking trails, picnic areas, playgrounds, and sports fields.

Forest Park is home to several world-class attractions, including:
- St. Louis Zoo: One of the nation's oldest and most respected zoos, the St. Louis Zoo is home to a diverse collection of animals from around the world. Visitors can see lions, tigers, elephants, giraffes, and many other species.
- Missouri Botanical Garden: This world-renowned botanical garden features stunning gardens, conservatories, and a vibrant research program. Visitors can explore themed gardens, such as the Japanese Garden, the Chinese Garden, and the Rose Garden.
- St. Louis Art Museum: The St. Louis Art Museum houses a vast collection of art from around the world, spanning centuries and cultures. Visitors can see works by famous artists such as Picasso, Monet, and Van Gogh.

Forest Park is the site of many annual events and festivals, including:

- Shakespeare Festival St. Louis: This popular festival features performances of Shakespeare's plays in an outdoor setting.
- Fair St. Louis: A large Independence Day celebration featuring fireworks, food, and entertainment.
- Winterfest: A winter festival with ice skating, holiday lights, and festive activities.

Downtown St. Louis: A Vibrant Urban Center

Downtown St. Louis is a bustling hub of activity, offering a wide range of shopping, dining, and entertainment options. From historic landmarks to trendy boutiques and vibrant nightlife, there's something for everyone in this vibrant urban center.

Popular Shopping Areas
- Delmar Loop: This eclectic neighborhood is a must-visit for shoppers seeking unique finds. Explore vintage clothing stores like Ragged Rabbit, trendy boutiques like The Garment District, and specialty shops like The Record Exchange.
- The City Museum: This quirky museum is a popular destination for families and children. It features interactive exhibits, climbing structures, a rooftop playground, and even a Ferris wheel.

Historic Buildings and Landmarks
- Old Courthouse: This historic building served as the federal courthouse for the St. Louis area and was the site of the famous Dred Scott case. Take a guided tour to learn about its significant role in American history.
- Union Station: A stunning historic train station that has been transformed into a mixed-use development. Enjoy dining, shopping, and entertainment options in this beautiful building.
- Eads Bridge: This iconic steel arch bridge connects St. Louis to East St. Louis, Illinois. Take a walk or bike ride across the bridge to enjoy panoramic views of the Mississippi River.

Nightlife and Entertainment Options

Downtown St. Louis offers a vibrant nightlife scene with a variety of bars, clubs, and live music venues. Popular entertainment options include:

- Ballpark Village: A sports and entertainment complex located near Busch Stadium, home of the St. Louis Cardinals. Enjoy live music, games, and delicious food in this vibrant atmosphere.
- Fox Theatre: A historic theater that hosts concerts, plays, and other performances. Catch a show by a world-renowned artist or enjoy a classic Broadway musical.
- The Pageant: A popular music venue that features a diverse lineup of bands and artists. Check the schedule to see who's playing during your visit.

Downtown St. Louis is a must-visit destination for anyone looking for a vibrant and exciting experience. With its diverse shopping options, historic landmarks, and lively nightlife, there's always something new to discover in this bustling urban center.

Ballpark Village: A Sports and Entertainment Hub

Ballpark Village is a vibrant destination located adjacent to Busch Stadium, home of the St. Louis Cardinals. This entertainment district offers a variety of restaurants, bars, and entertainment venues, making it a popular spot for sports fans and visitors alike.

As the home of the St. Louis Cardinals, Ballpark Village is a must-visit destination for baseball fans. Catch a game at Busch Stadium and experience the electric atmosphere of Cardinals baseball.

Ballpark Village offers a wide range of dining and entertainment options:
- Restaurants: Enjoy delicious food from a variety of cuisines, including burgers, pizza, tacos, and more. Popular restaurants include Cardinals Club, Budweiser Brewhouse, and Fox Sports Midwest Grill.
- Bars: Relax and enjoy a cold beer or a signature cocktail at one of Ballpark Village's many bars. Watch the game on a large screen TV or enjoy live music.
- Entertainment Venues: Ballpark Village hosts a variety of events throughout the year, including concerts, festivals, and family-friendly activities. Check the website for upcoming events.

Ballpark Village offers a variety of events and promotions throughout the year, including:
- Cardinals Baseball Games: Catch a game and experience the excitement of Cardinals baseball.
- Concerts: Enjoy live music from popular bands and artists.
- Festivals: Celebrate holidays and special occasions with festivals and events.
- Promotions: Take advantage of special offers and promotions, such as happy hour specials, food and drink deals, and giveaways.

Ballpark Village is a must-visit destination for anyone looking for a fun and exciting experience in St. Louis. With its world-class sports stadium, delicious food, and vibrant entertainment options, there's something for everyone to enjoy.

Soulard: A Historic Neighborhood with French Quarter Vibes

Soulard is a historic neighborhood in St. Louis known for its French Quarter-inspired atmosphere, charming architecture, and vibrant nightlife. This lively area offers a unique blend of history, culture, and entertainment.

Soulard was originally settled by French immigrants in the late 18th century, and its French heritage is still evident today. The neighborhood features narrow streets, brick buildings, and wrought-iron balconies, reminiscent of the French Quarter in New Orleans.

Soulard is home to a variety of restaurants, bars, and shops, offering something for every taste. Visitors can find a wide range of culinary options, from casual eateries to fine dining establishments. Popular restaurants and bars in Soulard include:

- Soulard Market: A historic indoor market featuring a variety of vendors selling fresh produce, meats, cheeses, and prepared foods.
- The Original Canteen: A popular restaurant serving St. Louis-style barbecue and other Southern comfort food.
- The Sidewalk Cafe: A cozy cafe offering a variety of coffee drinks, pastries, and sandwiches.
- The Boiler Room: A lively bar and music venue with a laid-back atmosphere.

Soulard also offers a variety of shops, including antique stores, boutiques, and gift shops.

Soulard is best known for its annual Mardi Gras celebration, one of the largest in the country. The celebration features colorful parades, live music, food vendors, and plenty of revelry. Mardi Gras in Soulard is a must-see event for anyone visiting St. Louis during the spring.

Soulard is a charming and vibrant neighborhood that offers a unique experience for visitors to St. Louis. With its historic architecture, diverse dining and entertainment options, and lively atmosphere, Soulard is a must-visit destination.

Tower Grove Park

Tower Grove Park is a beautiful and expansive urban park located in St. Louis. This serene oasis offers visitors a chance to escape the hustle and bustle of the city and enjoy nature at its finest.

Tower Grove Park features a variety of landscapes, including gardens, trails, and a lake. Visitors can stroll through the formal gardens, explore the wooded areas, or take a leisurely walk around the lake. The park is also home to a variety of wildlife, including birds, squirrels, and deer.

Some of the highlights of Tower Grove Park include:
- Japanese Garden: A peaceful and serene garden featuring traditional Japanese elements, such as a koi pond, stone lanterns, and a tea house.
- Conservatory: This glass-enclosed structure houses a variety of tropical plants and flowers.
- Trails: The park offers a variety of trails for walking, running, and biking.
- Lake: Visitors can rent boats or simply enjoy the scenic views of the lake.

Tower Grove Park is the site of many annual events and festivals, including:
- Tower Grove Park Summer Festival: A popular summer festival featuring live music, food vendors, and family-friendly activities.

- Shakespeare Festival St. Louis: This annual festival features performances of Shakespeare's plays in an outdoor setting.
- Tower Grove Park Winter Festival: A winter festival with ice skating, holiday lights, and festive activities.

Tower Grove Park is a must-visit destination for anyone seeking a peaceful and relaxing escape in the heart of St. Louis. With its beautiful gardens, trails, and lake, this park offers a unique and enjoyable experience for visitors of all ages.

The City Museum: A Quirky and Interactive Experience

The City Museum is a unique and interactive museum that is a popular destination for families and children. Located in St. Louis, Missouri, this quirky museum offers a variety of exhibits and attractions that are sure to spark the imagination.

The City Museum is housed in a historic shoe factory building, and its exhibits are designed to be both educational and entertaining. Visitors can climb through a giant monkey cage, slide down a 10-story slide, explore a maze of tunnels, and even crawl through a cave. The museum is also home to a rooftop playground, which offers stunning views of the city.

The City Museum is a popular destination for families and children due to its interactive and engaging exhibits. Kids of all ages will enjoy exploring the museum's many attractions and learning about a variety of topics, from art and science to history and architecture.

Anheuser-Busch Brewery: A Brewery Tour and Tasting Experience

Anheuser-Busch Brewery is a historic brewery located in St. Louis, Missouri. The brewery is home to Budweiser beer, one of the most popular beers in the world. Visitors can take a tour of the brewery and learn about the history of Budweiser and the brewing process.

Brewery tours at Anheuser-Busch offer visitors a behind-the-scenes look at the brewing process. Visitors can see how hops, barley, and yeast are combined to create Budweiser beer. At the end of the tour, visitors can enjoy a tasting of Budweiser and other Anheuser-Busch beers.

Anheuser-Busch is also home to the Clydesdale stables. These majestic horses are famous for their appearance in Budweiser commercials. Visitors can tour the stables and learn about the history of Clydesdale horses.

Anheuser-Busch Brewery is a great destination for beer lovers and those interested in learning about the brewing process. Visitors can enjoy a tour, tasting, and the opportunity to see the famous Clydesdale horses.

Neighborhoods to Explore: A Diverse St. Louis Experience

St. Louis offers a variety of neighborhoods, each with its own unique character and charm. From vibrant arts districts to historic neighborhoods and bustling commercial centers, there's something for everyone to explore.

Grand Center: Arts and Entertainment District

Grand Center is a thriving arts and entertainment district located just west of downtown St. Louis. This vibrant neighborhood is home to several world-class cultural institutions, including:

- St. Louis Symphony Orchestra: Enjoy a world-class performance at Powell Hall, home of the St. Louis Symphony Orchestra.
- Opera Theatre of Saint Louis: Experience the magic of opera at the Opera Theatre of Saint Louis.
- St. Louis Contemporary Art Museum: Explore contemporary art from around the world at this innovative museum.

- Fox Theatre: Catch a Broadway show or concert at this historic theater.

In addition to its cultural offerings, Grand Center also features a variety of restaurants, bars, and shops. The neighborhood is a great place to enjoy a meal, grab a drink, or catch a show.

Central West End: Upscale Shopping and Dining

Central West End is a trendy neighborhood known for its upscale shopping and dining options. This upscale district is home to a variety of boutiques, department stores, and specialty shops. Visitors can also find a wide range of restaurants, from casual eateries to fine dining establishments.

Some of the popular shopping and dining destinations in Central West End include:
- The Loop: A pedestrian-friendly shopping district with a variety of stores and restaurants.
- The Plaza: A mixed-use development featuring upscale shops, restaurants, and apartments.
- The Cheshire: A historic hotel that is home to several restaurants and bars.

Clayton: Suburban Neighborhood with Shops and Restaurants
Clayton is a suburban neighborhood located just west of St. Louis. This affluent area offers a variety of shops, restaurants, and parks. Visitors can explore the Clayton Plaza, a shopping center with a

variety of stores and restaurants. Clayton is also home to the Missouri Botanical Garden, a world-renowned botanical garden.

The Loop: Historic Neighborhood with Restaurants and Bars

The Loop is a historic neighborhood located in downtown St. Louis. This vibrant area is known for its diverse mix of restaurants, bars, and shops. Visitors can find a variety of culinary options, from casual eateries to fine dining establishments. The Loop is also a popular destination for nightlife, with a variety of bars and clubs.

Cherokee Street: Diverse Neighborhood with Shops, Restaurants, and Nightlife

Cherokee Street is a diverse neighborhood that offers a unique blend of culture, history, and entertainment. This vibrant area is home to a variety of shops, restaurants, and nightlife options. Visitors can explore the Cherokee Street Market, a historic indoor market with a variety of vendors. Cherokee Street is also a popular destination for live music, with several bars and clubs featuring local bands.

These are just a few of the many neighborhoods that St. Louis has to offer. Each neighborhood has its own unique character and charm, making it a great place to explore and discover.

24

chapter

04

Food and Drink

St. Louis is a city renowned for its diverse and delicious culinary scene. From iconic local specialties to world-class cuisine, there's something to satisfy every palate.

Local Specialties

- St. Louis-style barbecue: St. Louis is famous for its signature barbecue, which is typically made with pork ribs or pulled pork. The meat is slow-cooked in a sweet and smoky sauce, often served with french fries or coleslaw. Some of the best places to try St. Louis-style barbecue include Pappy's Smokehouse, Bogart's Smokehouse, and Gus's World Famous Fried Chicken.
    - Pappy's Smokehouse: This iconic St. Louis barbecue joint is known for its slow-cooked, fall-off-the-bone ribs and pulled pork. The restaurant has a casual atmosphere and is often crowded, but it's worth the wait for the delicious food.

- Bogart's Smokehouse: Another popular St. Louis barbecue spot, Bogart's Smokehouse offers a variety of barbecue meats, including ribs, pulled pork, and brisket. The restaurant also has a full bar and a live music stage.
- Gus's World Famous Fried Chicken: While not strictly barbecue, Gus's World Famous Fried Chicken is another popular St. Louis food destination. The restaurant serves crispy, juicy fried chicken that is sure to satisfy any craving.
- Gooey butter cake: This decadent dessert is a St. Louis institution. It's a dense, rich cake made with butter, sugar, and eggs, topped with a gooey layer of butter and powdered sugar. Gooey butter cake is a must-try for any visitor to St. Louis.
- Toasted ravioli: This unique appetizer is a St. Louis specialty. It consists of ravioli filled with meat or cheese, dipped in egg batter, and pan-fried until golden brown. Toasted ravioli is often served with marinara sauce or a spicy dipping sauce.
- Beefsteak sandwiches: Beefsteak sandwiches are another popular St. Louis dish. These hearty sandwiches are made with thinly sliced beefsteak, grilled onions, and provolone cheese, served on a toasted hoagie roll.
- Ice cream at Ted Drewes: Ted Drewes is a legendary St. Louis ice cream shop known for its frozen custard. The shop offers a variety of flavors, including chocolate, vanilla, and strawberry. Ted Drewes is a must-visit for any ice cream lover.

Best Restaurants

- Fine dining options: For a luxurious dining experience, visit one of St. Louis' many fine dining restaurants. The Tavern at the Four Seasons Hotel is a popular choice for upscale cuisine, while Brasserie Lafayette offers French-inspired fare.
- Casual eateries: St. Louis offers a variety of casual eateries, from casual diners to trendy food trucks. The Original Canteen is a popular spot for St. Louis-style barbecue, while The Loop Restaurant offers a diverse menu of American cuisine.
- Ethnic food: St. Louis is home to a diverse population, and this is reflected in its cuisine. Visitors can find a variety of ethnic restaurants, including Chinese, Italian, Mexican, and Vietnamese. Some popular ethnic restaurants in St. Louis include Baan Thai, Pastaria, El Taquito, and Pho Grand.

Breweries and Wineries

- Local craft beer scene: St. Louis has a thriving craft beer scene, with many breweries producing high-quality beers. Popular breweries include Urban Chestnut Brewing Company, Schlafly Beer Company, and 4 Hands Brewing Company.
- Missouri wine regions: Missouri is home to several wine regions, including the Missouri River Valley and the Ozark Mountains. Visitors can take tours of wineries and sample local wines. Some popular Missouri wineries include Stone Hill Winery, Bur Oak Winery, and Al Mar Vineyard.
  - St. Louis offers a diverse and delicious culinary scene that is sure to satisfy any palate. From iconic local specialties to world-class cuisine, there's something for everyone to enjoy.

Outdoor Activities in St. Louis

St. Louis offers a variety of outdoor activities for visitors to enjoy, from hiking and biking to boating and fishing. Here are some of the best options:

Hiking and Biking Trails
Forest Park: This sprawling urban park offers a variety of trails for hiking and biking. Visitors can explore the park's wooded areas, lakes, and gardens.
Riverfront Trail: This paved trail follows the Mississippi River and offers beautiful views of the city.
Castlewood State Park: Located just west of St. Louis, Castlewood State Park offers a variety of hiking and biking trails, as well as a lake for fishing and boating.

Boating and Fishing
Mississippi River: The Mississippi River offers opportunities for

boating, fishing, and paddleboarding. Visitors can rent boats or kayaks from several locations along the riverfront.

Lake Chesterfield: This large lake is located just west of St. Louis and offers opportunities for boating, fishing, and swimming.

Castlewood State Park: In addition to hiking and biking, Castlewood State Park also offers opportunities for boating and fishing on its lake.

Golf Courses

St. Louis is home to several golf courses, offering a variety of challenges and scenery. Some of the best golf courses in the area include:

Whitaker Hills Golf Course: This public golf course is located in Forest Park and offers a challenging 18-hole course.

Gateway National Golf Links: This public golf course is located near Lambert International Airport and offers stunning views of the city.

Whitaker Park Golf Course: This private golf course is known for its well-maintained greens and challenging layout.

Whether you're looking for a leisurely walk in the park or an adrenaline-pumping adventure, St. Louis offers a variety of outdoor activities to suit your interests.

Cultural Events in St. Louis

St. Louis is a vibrant city with a rich cultural scene. Visitors can enjoy a variety of cultural events, including museums, galleries, theaters, and festivals.

Museums and Galleries
- St. Louis Art Museum: This world-class museum features a vast collection of art from around the world, spanning centuries and cultures.
- Missouri Botanical Garden: A botanical garden with stunning gardens, conservatories, and a vibrant research program.
- St. Louis Science Center: A hands-on science museum with interactive exhibits for all ages.
- Gateway Arch Museum: Learn about the history of the Gateway Arch and the westward expansion of the United States.
- The City Museum: A quirky and interactive museum with unique exhibits and attractions.

Theaters and Performing Arts
- Opera Theatre of Saint Louis: Enjoy world-class opera performances at this renowned theater.
- St. Louis Symphony Orchestra: Listen to classical music performed by one of the world's leading orchestras.
- Fox Theatre: Catch a Broadway show or concert at this historic theater.
- Repertory Theatre of St. Louis: Enjoy professional theater productions at this regional theater.

Festivals and Events
- Fair St. Louis: A large Independence Day celebration featuring fireworks, food, and entertainment.
- Shakespeare Festival St. Louis: Enjoy performances of Shakespeare's plays in an outdoor setting.
- St. Louis Blues Hockey Season: Cheer on the St. Louis Blues, the city's professional hockey team.
- St. Louis Cardinals Baseball Season: Watch a game at Busch Stadium, home of the St. Louis Cardinals.
- Missouri Botanical Garden's Flower Festival: Enjoy beautiful floral displays and gardens during this annual festival.

St. Louis offers a wide variety of cultural events for visitors to enjoy. Whether you're interested in art, music, theater, or history, there's something for everyone in this vibrant city.

Family-Friendly Activities in St. Louis

St. Louis offers a variety of family-friendly activities that are sure to keep kids entertained. Here are some popular options:

Zoos and Aquariums

- St. Louis Zoo: One of the nation's oldest and most respected zoos, the St. Louis Zoo is home to a diverse collection of animals from around the world. Visitors can see lions, tigers, elephants, giraffes, and many other species.
- St. Louis Aquarium at Union Station: This aquarium features a variety of marine life, including sharks, sea turtles, and tropical fish. Visitors can also enjoy interactive exhibits and touch tanks.

Children's Museums

- St. Louis Science Center: This hands-on science museum offers a variety of interactive exhibits that are perfect for children of all ages.

- Magic House at the Muny: This children's museum features interactive exhibits that encourage creativity and learning.
- Kiddo! Children's Museum: This museum offers a variety of exhibits and activities for young children.

Amusement Parks
- Six Flags St. Louis: This amusement park offers a variety of thrill rides, roller coasters, and water slides.
- Six Flags Hurricane Harbor St. Louis: This water park features a variety of water slides, wave pools, and lazy rivers.

St. Louis offers a variety of family-friendly activities that are sure to keep kids entertained. Whether you're looking for educational experiences or thrilling adventures, there's something for everyone in this vibrant city.

Practical Information for Your St. Louis Trip

Getting Around

St. Louis offers a variety of transportation options for visitors. Here's a breakdown of the most common methods:

Public Transportation
- MetroLink: The MetroLink is a light rail system that serves St. Louis and its suburbs. It connects major attractions, including the Gateway Arch, Forest Park, and the downtown area. Single-ride fares are available, as well as day passes and weekly passes.
- Buses: St. Louis has a network of city buses that serve various neighborhoods and attractions. Single-ride fares are available, as well as day passes and weekly passes.

Taxis and Ride-Sharing Services
Taxis and ride-sharing services like Uber and Lyft are readily

available in St. Louis. You can hail a taxi on the street or use a smartphone app to request a ride.

Car Rental
If you prefer to have your own transportation, you can rent a car at St. Louis Lambert International Airport or at various locations throughout the city. Driving in St. Louis is relatively easy, and there are plenty of parking garages and lots available.

Accommodation
St. Louis offers a variety of accommodation options to suit different budgets and preferences. Here are some examples:

Hotels and Resorts
St. Louis has a wide range of hotels and resorts, from budget-friendly options to luxury accommodations. Some popular hotels include:
- Four Seasons Hotel St. Louis: A luxury hotel located in the Central West End neighborhood.
- The Ritz-Carlton St. Louis: A historic hotel located downtown, offering elegant accommodations and world-class amenities.
- The Chase Park Plaza: A grand hotel located in the Central West End neighborhood, featuring a rooftop pool and spa.

Bed and Breakfasts
For a more intimate and personalized experience, consider staying at a bed and breakfast. St. Louis has several charming bed and breakfasts located in historic neighborhoods throughout the city.

Vacation Rentals
If you're looking for a more homey atmosphere, consider renting a vacation home or apartment. Websites like Airbnb and Vrbo offer a variety of options in St. Louis.

Safety Tips
St. Louis, like any large city, has areas with higher crime rates. It's important to be aware of your surroundings and take necessary precautions. Here are some safety tips:
- Stay in well-lit and populated areas at night.
- Avoid walking alone in unfamiliar neighborhoods.
- Be cautious when using ATMs.
- Don't leave valuables unattended in public places.
- If you feel unsafe, call 911 immediately.
- By following these tips, you can help ensure a safe and enjoyable trip to St. Louis.

Glossary
of Local Terms

Gooey butter cake: A rich and decadent dessert made with butter, sugar, and eggs.

Toasted ravioli: A St. Louis specialty consisting of ravioli dipped in egg batter and pan-fried.

Beefsteak sandwich: A hearty sandwich made with thinly sliced beefsteak, grilled onions, and provolone cheese.

St. Louis-style barbecue: Barbecue made with pork ribs or pulled pork, slow-cooked in a sweet and smoky sauce.

Delmar Loop: A vibrant neighborhood known for its eclectic shops, restaurants, and entertainment venues.

Central West End: An upscale neighborhood with a variety of boutiques, department stores, and restaurants.

Clayton: A suburban neighborhood with shops, restaurants, and parks.

The Loop: A historic neighborhood downtown, known for its diverse mix of restaurants, bars, and shops.

Cherokee Street: A diverse neighborhood with shops, restaurants, and nightlife.

Gateway Arch: An iconic stainless steel monument symbolizing the westward expansion of the United States.

Forest Park: A large urban park with a variety of attractions, including the St. Louis Zoo, Missouri Botanical Garden, and Art Museum.

Ballpark Village: A sports and entertainment complex located near Busch Stadium, home of the St. Louis Cardinals.

Soulard: A historic neighborhood with French Quarter vibes, known for its annual Mardi Gras celebration.

Tower Grove Park: A beautiful park with gardens, trails, and a lake.

MetroLink: The light rail system that serves St. Louis and its suburbs.

Quotes
about St. Louis

"St. Louis is a city that's got a lot of heart. It's a city that's got a lot of history. And it's a city that's got a lot of soul." - T.J. Oshie, former St. Louis Blues hockey player

"St. Louis is a great place to raise a family. It's got a great school system, it's got a great quality of life, and it's got a great community." - Stan Musial, former St. Louis Cardinals baseball player

"St. Louis is a city that's always been good to me. It's a city that's given me so much." - Nelly, rapper and St. Louis native

"St. Louis is a city of contrasts. It's a city of tradition and innovation. It's a city of old and new." - Mayor Tishaura Jones

"St. Louis is a city that's full of surprises. You never know what you're going to find around the next corner." - Anonymous

"St. Louis is a city that's got a great food scene. You can find anything you want to eat here." - Michael Pollan, author and food activist

"St. Louis is a city that's got a great music scene. There's always something going on." - Chuck Berry, rock and roll pioneer

"St. Louis is a city that's got a great sports scene. We've got the Cardinals, the Blues, and the Rams." - John Madden, sportscaster

"St. Louis is a city that's got a great arts scene. There's always something new to see and do." - Nina Simone, singer and civil rights activist

"St. Louis is a city that's got a great history. There's so much to learn about this place." - Doris Kearns Goodwin, historian

"St. Louis is a city that's got a great spirit. The people here are friendly and welcoming." - Maya Angelou, poet and civil rights activist

"St. Louis is a city that's got a great future. I'm excited to see what the future holds for this place." - Jon Hamm, actor

"St. Louis is a city that's got a great vibe. It's a city that's got a lot of energy." - Pharrell Williams, musician and producer

St. Louis,
A City Worth Exploring

St. Louis is a vibrant and diverse city that offers something for everyone. From its iconic landmarks to its thriving cultural scene, there's always something new to discover.

Whether you're a history buff, a foodie, or simply seeking a relaxing getaway, St. Louis is a must-visit destination. With its friendly locals, beautiful parks, and unique attractions, this city is sure to leave a lasting impression.

Thank you for choosing St. Louis as your destination! I hope this guide has been helpful in planning your trip.

Happy travels!

J.B. Daniels

Made in United States
Troutdale, OR
02/12/2025

28931161R00037